THE SCRIBBLES
OF MY
BROKEN LIFE

Regina Ducey

I pour out my heart
To anyone who's left more tears on the bathroom floor
than dirty laundry...
To anyone who's had anger burning within from all of
the shit they've been through...
To those who have tried to diminish our light,
and to those who have stayed by our sides during the
darkest of hours.
This is for you
For us

My life has been filled with trauma after trauma, drama after drama. As a child I was a product of my surroundings, living with a pain and suffering that I could not control. Fast forward to being an adult; my surroundings became a product of me.. Sad, lonely, sick. I was holding onto over 30 years of trauma. This led to bad relationships filled with narcissism, sadness, deceit, abuse - you name it! Illnesses that have crippled me for way too long, leaving me immobile at times, and let's not forget the heaping amount of pain both emotionally and physically. I started to write as a way to release some of the things rattling around in my head. The things I was never able to say out loud. Putting them onto paper was like taking a breath of fresh air after not being able to breathe for some time. So, I started to breathe! I had been holding my breath for nearly 30 years! Once my fingers began to bleed out all of the things I no longer needed to keep, I began to see and feel more clearly. It was the beginning of my healing. Soon after, I decided to put all of my work into my books. I am moving forward, putting all of the past traumas, heartache, and losses to rest. I say good-bye to all that I've allowed to hold me back and share my strength with the World. I have gotten through 100% of the bad moments and hard times. Thank you for joining me as I scribble my way through the madness.

⟨moon symbol⟩

Disclaimer:
This book is filled with events that can be triggering. Read with caution and if you feel overwhelmed by your emotions, contact your Doctor, Therapist, or Local Hotline. Sending Love and Light to you!

My Poetry

The beginning I do not start
but I dive right into the deep
the deepest parts of my heart
I'll tear these pages apart

My words here are formed
take them and see past them
I must take a moment to warn
deep feelings and thoughts
are pressed within the hem

CHAPTER 1
I BEGIN

Writing's Of My Soul

It doesn't come easy
these words that I write
all filled with emotions
all filled with insight

To write down my soul
an easy task one may think
all these bruised words
like pieces to my broken link

So slow and so heavy
so deep and true
these words I write
I'll never be able to undo

Let the Story in

As the words pour from my mouth
tears begin to fall
Telling my story becomes harder

I push through the tears
open up
place that story upon the shelf

Who I was
no longer is me

As my story changes daily
I let everyone in
let them all see
This story will not define me

IT IS WHΛT IT IS

Everything that has happened to me
is My story
I'm going to write my story!
If you wanted me to write
sweet stories about how you are wonderful
Then you should have
behaved better!

Me

I've been broke
I've been beat
I've been burned

I've seen what cannot be unseen
having very few to lean
Getting by so very strong
knowing what's right
what's wrong

Telling you who I am
helps break down this defense program
After all I've been through
there's just so much to get into

Beautiful Imperfections

Beautifully unbeautiful words
lay across this page
I lay them out here
with so much to gain
As I sit here
with this ache in my heart
I hold myself up
try my best to not fall apart
Twenty-nine years
the wounds have not healed
Twenty-nine years worth
 I've tried to conceal
None of which
I've found that works
So I lose myself
in my beautifully tragic artwork
I find the perfection
in the imperfections
And find no need
to make any corrections
This terribly sad and painful life is echoing   ➜

I feel its lifeforce ever so connecting
I'll use everything that's happened to me
To push me forward
undoubtedly

Overthinking is My Talent

Noticing everything
is exhausting

It leads to my ability to really overthink things
and for that
I am a pro

WHO WOULD I BE?

What if...

What if I let go of all the heartache I've ever felt?
What if I leave all the daily pain behind?
What if my heart didn't race everytime I walked into a full room?
What if I didn't care what others thought of me?
What would be left?
Who would I even be?

Mad Hatter

While they point their fingers at me
with disgust in their eyes
shouting
"Black Sheep!"

I sit upon the throne they have given me
wearing my crooked hat
with a sly smile on my face..
"I'm no black sheep!
I'm a
Mad Hatter!!"

To Protect My Empathy

I try
and
I try again
Somehow
I come back to this
I can feel
the entire World's sin
I fear
there's nothing I miss

Because I feel things
so intense
and I can see
what's left unseen
I have to put up
quite the defense
to keep my broken soul
clean

Δ Heavy Drought

Lately my words have gone blank
I've become more angry
My soul feels like it sank
My goddess
more hungry

This woman I used to know
disappeared before my eyes
On the outside it may not show
Deep down I'm filled with heavy cries

The days go by so empty
I try so hard to not scream out
For now I'll let my soul be
Riding the waves of this drought

Dismissing Me

I don't know her anymore
she left without a word
All that time being ignored
she was feeling so unheard

Her heart torn and lost
her soul bleeding out through her skin
I never really knew the full cost
what would happen if she did not fit in

The pain sat on her sleeve
as the torture fled from her eyes
Her loss I will forever grieve
To remember I'll forever try

Was she ever a reality
Did she actually exist
This woman I talk of is me
This woman I've always dismissed

Exploring My Essence

Sitting in this aching agony
I sit alone..
From the ashes I have risen
Covered in the blood of my atoned
With my shadow by my side
I start to see it's potential
Catching my flooding cries
my life's essence is essential
The dark from which I came
doesn't phase me anymore
What once was my fear
I've now learned to explore

Free

A tortured soul
that's what I see
Life's taken its toll
I do not feel as if I am free

One day at a time
One crisis after the next
My life feels like a crime
My life is such a mess

I say hello
with a quick good-bye
It's out of my control
The shortness of life we can't deny

I have grown so tired
I just want to rest
As my brain rewires
I lose my protest

THIRSTY

My mind never sleeps
It's dehydrated
Searching for rain
in a drought filled desert

TODAY'S CHAOS

Such a fast paced world
gnawing at my heart
Sending it into overdrive
Tearing it apart

So much hate ripping
at my inner peace
There's nowhere to run
No time to weep

As I rush through today
feeling the panic all around
I can't seem to stay calm
I'm feeling all of the sounds

My soul begs me to slow
This life begs for chaos
There's nowhere to go
This whirlwind has caused so much loss

Boundaries

I love to help others
But my help
has no boundaries

I find myself
lost and hurt
Hands deep
in their issues

While I'm out at sea
drowning
They sit back and relax
just watching

You're a Control Freak!

Yeah
That's what happens when you grow up
having everything around you be
completely out of control!

In the Genetics

My father abandoned me
long before
he actually left
Maybe that's why
I cut every cord
before it's fully sewn

DRUNKEN PALACE

I live in a drunken palace
No one knows my name
They know nothing about me
I might as well be invisible

That would be too easy

"The fat girl!"
"The sarcastic mouth!"
"Too picky!"
"Too sad!"
"Too angry and mad!"

Words thrown
"Bitch!"
"Slut!"
"Whore!"
"No good!"

→

Questions asked
"Why are you even here?"
"Why do you cry so much?"
"Why do you act like that?"

Statements passed
"She's just a bitch!"
"Everyone has hard times!"
"She just wants attention!"
"She should have just left!"

My drunken palace
No one knows my name
They know nothing about me

My Life

It's as dark as night
as black as sin
I try to hold on with all my might
trying to not let it in

Sometimes it can be quiet
Sometimes it's so very loud
I'm forevermore trying to fight it
Even when it has no sound

It's round of neverending torment
takes me by surprise
I try to open up and vent
from my mouth it all sounds of lies

This situation I am talking about
it's not simple really at all
I can't live without
without it I surely will fall

➜

This revelation is called my life
my life
so very dark
The tension could be cut with a knife
it's definitely left its mark

My life has been just this
Catastrophic events and misfortunes
It's something easily missed
if you don't have the right absorption

THE SEARCH

The universe swallows me whole
I fight to survive
In search deep within my soul
for that spark to revive
My cries for help
Silenced
My cries
Erased
Any help turns into violence
my soul is being replaced
This search will just continue
until I get what I need
I will search for an open window
for my moment to be freed

Δ New Light

The warm inviting sun
beams right off my face
a bright sparkle of a new day
I quiet this overcrowded mind
that starts to race
it pleads
trying to have its own way
I just don't live there anymore
that dark unforgiving place of disappointment
With my inner strength
I picked myself up off the floor
I found the beauty in still moments
The deep meanings of each day
the beauty in tomorrow
The serendipity of today
I've learned to never push away my sorrow
If so it shows in a negative way
demanding to be felt
So I embrace what every little bit has to say
I work with what I'm dealt

"I'M FINE"

"I'm fine"
I say as if I'm trying to convince myself
Watering myself down like an overgrown garden of
chaos
The words slip from my tongue
like they were destined for this sentence
Put to the time until I reach my repentance
How easy I lose myself
in the vocabulary from my darkened past
Hateful words wrapped in the vines of my mind
to remember at long last
Lies drenched with more lies
spewing hatred at it's every turn
I lie to myself
after you lie to me
I've caught on
I'm ready to learn
Take my distressed Heart
and listen to it's last beat
How quickly "I'm Fine"
turned into my very own defeat ➔

The anguish drips
like the faucet to my soul
Sending it unstable disputes
to ricochet leaving me troubled
I cling to the lie
that's dripping from my lips
The apocalypse of "I'm Fine"
sends my World into an eclipse

An Empire of Darkness

The quiet words
are screaming so loud
I look down
from upon my dark cloud
I can see the hidden pain
your trying to deliver
That darkness reaches me
I start to quiver
I'll take all of this pain
with such a harsh guilt
After all
this is the empire I've built
Happiness will never
radiate from me
My broken past
and dark future
are all that I am able see

Built Tolerance

I'm witty
Sometimes abrasive
I've learned the hard way
that not everyone has thick skin

WHEN TOO MUCH BOTHERS YOU

You say I'm too much
Maybe it's time
you go find
Less

Contradictory Personality

Is there anyone out there?
Hello?
I'm drowning from within
I just can't seem to let it go
I'm feeling so defeated
I can't take this pain
of feeling so alone
living in shame
I just want to go home
Why can't I come out
step into the sun
let myself feel
have a little fun
This prison is so lonely
being in here all alone
living in the dark
the light has never shown
I'm too scared to open the door
not knowing what's on the other side
I can't take the risk
I'd rather stay here and hide

➜

But I want to get out
please tell me what to do
Anything has to be easier
than this
contradictory attitude

Chapter 2
MEDICAL

I never realized just how far I could be pushed until I was pushed a whole lot

Δ DΔϒ IN Mϒ LIᴘе

The ache in my neck
the fullness in my head
I feel like a wreck
I've forgotten the words I just said

My legs, how they hurt
My hands pins and needles
I may have to just blurt
how this pain feels so evil

My words come in a stutter
I'm losing my sight
My head feels so cluttered
I'm pushing on with all my might

My legs how they give
my feet out of sync
I have a strong will to live
I just want to sever this link

→

Take all this pain
Take all these strifes
Just leave me sane
Give me back my life

Let Go

The truth spreads across my tainted skin
it's left for all to see
This blood boils so deep within
this soul scream's 'Let me Be'

I sit here in such agony
I sit here full of pain
Clouded rain days are all I see
a drought would be such a gain

My insides are just crying out
this vessels skin to harsh
My soul shakes and shouts
it's in search within for a spark

My head is so full
I just can't keep up
I wish to just let go
of this vessel and all of its ruts

Let it All Go

My heart
hurting intensely
My mind
clouded
numb
This isn't how it's meant to be
I can't change where I come from
My eyes
blurred with tainted cries
My soul
aches
Going through all the lies
Going through the mistakes
Push this away
as it makes me feel so crushed
and broken
See things more clearly
let go of the toxic words spoken

Erupting Ache

The ache...
Deep and discrete
Races from ground to peak
It's raw need to extinguish a positive day
so unparalleled and leading astray
The sting is causing such distress
a tornado of nagging depress
It devours my very essence
with deep screams and incessant questions
It builds like lava waiting to erupt
I can't give in now
I can't give up

TODAY'S ANXIETY

This knife in my chest
has turned a bit more
My head in my hands
I come crashing to the floor
My stomach in knots
my head how it spins
I can't seem to focus
It's all flooding in
A handful of issues
lay right at my feet
They block me from moving
I'm feeling defeat
Now the worlds turning dark
I can't catch my breath
I have to push away
this tiring mess
I fear if I don't
I'll forever be
Stuck here
in my anxiety

WHΛT THE MIND CΛN'T BELIEVE

There's something in the pain that I feel
something that is so condescending
I sit here and wonder if this pains even real
or is it my mind just mending

I've been through Hell most of my life
not knowing how to face it
Day by day living in strife
I'm just so tired of this shit

I wake up feeling such distress
my body aching
my mind feeling rushed
I tell myself this is my ultimate test
My soul tells my body to hush

I go day by day
pretending to be okay
It's not a lie if you truly believe it
My soul is telling me what I need to say
but my mind feels like an endless empty pit

Feeling

I pull myself up
from the bed where I sleep
It's never enough
and I'm left here to weep
No matter how I try
it's always the same
My face tells a lie
All I'm feeling
is shame

Fleeing from Invisible Fear

My veins are screaming
with passion to flee
My heart pounding so loudly
from the outside can be seen
My palms
so sweaty
shaking with fury
This flight in me
has me so worried
Fear has nestled down deep in my soul
It's making me feel
I just have to go
I'm trying to fight it
with all that I've got
This fear has me feeling
I'm something I'm not

INSΔNE

This dis-ease clings to my life like the tear soaked shirt
lays on my skin
This pain demands attention
I can't push it away
or
just ignore it
My body won't stand the rejection
With tears in my eyes
an ache so intense
I move forward all the same
deep down I feel I'm already dead
at the surface I feel insane

BLURR

Searching for hope felt almost ludicrous

asking for help

humiliating

Saying it outloud was so humorous

Their laughter

degrading

This torturing discomfort I feel

brings me insanity

Being told my pain isn't real

Where is the humanity?

Snuff out my light while beating me down

as if this pain is not enough

As my body continues to break down

they continue calling it a bluff

DR.

I sat in that white silent room
waiting on the cold bed
As I lay all my faults at your feet
I can't help but replay the last things you've said

As my mind starts to wander
your uncaring eyes coldly meet mine
I'm just another number
that continues to decline

You care less about my discomfort
as you send me away
A prescription in hand
seems to be the only way

Another day
another pill
It never matters what I say
for I must abide your will

➡

Standing at the sink
I swallow this pill whole
When will they find the link
These pills have taken their toll

Dried Flower

Drained
like an old dried up flower
my body aches and strains to get up
I wish for the strength as I feel like a coward
everyday I search for the power of luck

Today has been reaped and the cost is misery
I can't get out of my mind
the pain is undeniably
keeping me from being kind

This flower so crumpled
it hurts to move
My mind stays jumbled
as I watch the last dried up petal be removed

My Pain Today

This pain is cruel
I sit here in agony
Feeling of a fool
my brain wonders how this can be
The radiating pain
shoots through my body
driving me insane
I feel my head nodding
I can not stand
but it's much too painful to lay here
My pain has much to demand
now, on sets the fear
What do I do
with a pain so intense
It's really nothing new
So I must build a defense

DR-PATIENT CONFIDENTIALITY

I asked for help
They filled me full of toxins
never explaining of all the Harm
They told me I was crazy
sent me home without alarm

They said I was too heavy
never telling me how to be light
They treated me so cruel
I lost my burning will to fight

I kept going back with new complaints
they sent me for more tests
Diagnosis was now my restraint
I feared I'd never get any true rest

To follow this pain go back to the top
to that moment of vulnerability
I found that healing is an inside job
Going to them
kept me in captivity

A Choice in my Pain

That beating in my chest has changed
it's so fast
so fierce
My mind no longer keeps up with it
not everything is as it appears
The wind that blows on my skin
it is painful indeed
It matches the pain I feel inside
this pain I just want to relieve
The choice of none does not exist
I must keep going forward
I just can't seem to resist
the pain I always go toward

WILL I FIND MY FREEDOM

The taste of rusted nails
leaves me breathless
The feeling of bitterness
takes form
My broken body
has me guessing
During these times
I refuse to conform
Thoughts of better days
lay deep in my mind
So far away from me
I sit and wonder if I'll ever find
my chance to break through and be free

My Soul Wants More

My body
the vessel of wasteland
the home of my heart
put through more than I can stand
falling apart
This Soul wants more

My head
the space overfilled
so complicated and weak
I'm less than thrilled
tripping over the words I speak
This Soul wants more

My Heart
overloaded
sad and strong
outdated
beats to it's own song
This Soul wants more

➙

Me
pain of a thousand daggers
body
head
heart
My Soul aches for more

ΛBBREVIΛTIONS

She's left
then she's right
Sometimes up
mostly down
She's clinging on tight
to any drama around
Her mind how it spins
her heart starts to race
All the battles she tries to win
she still can't find her right place
The struggles so real
the pain just non stop
There's no time to heal
she feels she just can't keep up
To the depths she will take this
although not her fault
Such a painful thing to witness
together her body and mind assault

Δ Haircut

The hair fell to the floor so swiftly
my burnt out body sat still
My vision no longer sees clearly
Where do I find all of my will?

Layer by layer it goes
it's not for me anymore
The pain no one else knows
now some is left on the floor

My vessel is slowly giving in
to the disorders of the World
It can't live with the way of man's sin
slowly I'm taken to the netherworld

So for today I do what I can
to survive another day
I may never be ready for when
I'm left with absolutely no say

Misplaced Womb

I said goodbye to my womb
the place that couldn't hold you
I was already feeling so empty

I said goodbye to the pain
the deep jabs of fire
I was already over feeling

I said goodbye to whom I once was
so lost
thinking I was less than I am

I never needed the womb
that caused the pain
that left me feeling empty

It wasn't who I am
It wasn't who I was
It was just one small part of me

Chapter 3
MY EARLY YEARS

I avoided these parts of my life for so long, not understanding why they would pop up at random times. It was when I began working through the triggers that I was finally able to begin to heal.

She will Find Herself

Her tiny mind
broken with pain
She's left with fear
heartache
strain
Nothing seems
to make any sense
Feeling like her whole life
is such a big mess
Seeking for friendship
in all the wrong places
Has her believing
she has been misplaced
She screams
yells
begs for help
She can't seem to gain
control of herself
Locking her feelings
up so tight
Makes her scream out

→

with all of her might
One day she will
find who she really is
Standing tall
ignoring what everyone says

She'll be proud
Strong
Finally be herself
That strong little girl
who's been hiding deep down

Left

It started at a young age
a pattern it became
Growing into undealt rage
keeping me less sane

From every woman to man
Every family to friend
Making me feel banned
I was unable to comprehend

This open door policy
wasn't as cozy as you'd think
Everyone just left me
as quick as I could blink

How quickly they were here
How quickly they would go
Living in this fear
of when they'd leave
I didn't know

Fear of the Dark

they come in all shapes in sizes
they hide in plain sight
the truth can be alarming
you have to learn not to fight
do not kick
do not scream
just close your eyes
after all
it's just a bad dream
one day they'll all go away
leaving you utterly alone
after they've made you fall astray
your broken house will become your home
you cannot blame yourself you see
you cannot hold it all in
just hold your head up and let it be
never let them win
these monsters that dishonored you
they live in your head in all you do
they take that humiliation and feed on it
just never give up

→

never give in
in the end
you're the one with all the power
they're just small monsters
that hide in the dark
waiting to devour

Unanswered Questions

Where was my innocence lost

Was it the men who didn't care about **No**
In the bar filled with drunken mouths
Was it when his hand met my face
or was it the one wrapped around my throat

Was that innocence ever really there
or was it slowly ripped away
So many unanswered questions
to those who have nothing left to say

Pieces Left in Hiding Places

She was brilliant, beautiful
so full of life
Her secrets she clung to
wanting to bury them deep inside
No one would know
No one even cared
Her life was their show
her life so unfair
Her beautiful hiding places
so dark and so small
She'd bury herself there
where she felt she could get through it all
The pain that she felt everyday
was more then the pain being dealt
Leaving her in early decay
her soul she no longer felt
She'll hide away
hide from it all
These places she could forever stay
as they pick her up everytime she falls

Hiding Places

Dark places
Deep spaces
I was always at ease in those confined hiding places

No danger to me,
hiding behind a pitbull who wasn't scared of anyone.
Showing his teeth to let them know he wasnt fucking
around. We hid, tucked away from the true monsters of
my world in his compact little dog house.

No danger to me,
as I slid back my closet door converting the bright space
that homed my clothes into a dark dungeon of safety.

No danger to me,
when I slipped my small frail body under my bed,
covering my eyes from seeing the truth but listening to
the scream's down the hall.

→

No danger to me,
when the man with the needle protruding from his
marked arm remembered to lock me in a cold dark
room with a small window overlooking my freedom.
It was always safer in locked up, small dark spaces!
My hiding places!

It's Our Condition

And there we went, walking away. Actually it was more like running away from anything that could start to feel like home. Never looking back, always moving.

If we stop for too long we might catch some reality. So we keep running. Run so far that we can lose ourselves. Lose ourselves in the dramas of what to do next and where to go. Living life in chaos is all we've ever known.

This is it.

This is our way.

Who She Was

You never protected me when I was a child
you made me feel as if I was not worth your while
All those monsters that took my sanity
while you were out worried about your vanity
The screaming, the yelling, the begging for help
I was your child you should have helped yourself
You put it all on me to take care of everything
no care in the World of how bad that would sting
The endless men with the endless drinks
I'd hold back your hair as you left them all in the sink
As I have grown I've become very weary
You now have changed but I'll forever remember your
fury
All of those nights that I just could not sleep
have caught up to me as I sit here and weep
You are no longer that uncaring woman
but after twenty years it's all been deeply woven
After much time, you I will forgive
For you my mother, you have shown me my will to Live

LIFE ON THE FARM

On that farm is where my magic was put out
like heavy rain to a fire
Smoke filling the sky like the fear filled my heart
The smile that once laid upon my innocent face now
gone
The hands of pure evil wrapped around my tiny neck
Looking into the darkest of eyes
I saw no soul
a small amount of comfort that brought
As my body started to go limp
I stopped fighting
Darkness started to overcome
A cold thump upon my bottom
dropping me to the ground he walked away never
looking back
fear filled me as I lay and watch
As soon as the sight is clear I'm gone
Out to the barn I go
Trying to put back
the pieces of my puzzle that were just put through a
shredder

LIFE ON THE FARM PART 2

After being locked up for days
freedom was my reward
a play date with my cousin
After finding the babysitter
lifeless on the floor
chaos has now arisen
Laying there in her own blood
with the needle coming from her arm
we turned on the bath water

Taking everything in us we lifted her together
how quickly that water looked of horror
Her lifeless body still not moving
we stood there so still
so scared
no clues to what we're doing
our minds mentally impaired
With a gasp from her lungs she reached for the needle
now we could finally breathe
Was she not happy that the dose was not lethal?
This was true insanity

Banana Splits

Sitting at this table
with kids I do not know
All talking about their lives
in attempts to help us grow

The teacher sits and listens
taking notes on each of us
One by one down the line
there's much to discuss

It finally gets to me
it's my time to share my story
After listening to everyone else
my mind now feels so worried

I see the teacher and her notes
only writing when it's dramatic
I wonder what she'll do
it's feeling problematic

→

I've been here before
sharing my little secrets
Only they were not kept
and I was sent away for treatment

I do not share this time
I just smile and say my name
The teacher smiles and nods
she doesn't see my game

Why do they gather us
the ones with broken homes
Bring us in a secluded room
For others can now throw stones

They made it seem so special
like we were the winners of something
Only the broken kids
who come from nothing

→

They may have been trying to help
but it made us stand right out
The freaks who have only one parent
This began my road of doubt

Ignorant Love

Hands over my ears
hiding under my bed
as if this shelter was safety

The screams have me in fear
so many tears I've shed
this continues almost daily

How is this love?
This hate that's been thrown around
Do they even know the difference?
They'll continue to push and shove
until there's absolutely no sound
and live everyday in ignorance

THROWN

They threw each other around the living room as she begged me for help. Then they told each other how much they loved one another..
Now they wonder why I have trust issues.

Shhh

We dont talk about the rape that's been endured
we must keep it silent
It's best to just ignore
this unjustified violence
He can put his hand down her pants
if they're behind closed doors
Everyone knows just what's in his plans
he'll raise her like a whore
It's ok that he takes her perfect flower
leaving it bleeding on the bed
She'll wash away his sin in the coldest of showers
pushing these events out of her head

DARK

The tides turned when she found me
laying amongst the cold dried up lake
I shivered at her warmth
She whispered to me "Stand with strength."
I needed to find my worth
I left it there on the ground for everyone to walk on
Surrounded by darkness
Feeling completely
empty and dark

CHAPTER 4

LOSS

Grief changes over time, but it never goes away completely. Feeling a sadness so deep that it feels as if you could bleed out from the sorrow that's built up in you. Grief may have many colors, shapes, and smells but they all demand attention equally.

Δ Suffocating Choice

That memory popped up again
It streamed down my cheek building a river beneath my
feet
That very memory that hurts so fucking much
It's trying to drown me
I won't let it go but I hate that suffocating feeling
The obvious choice seems terribly hard
Here I float in the tears of the past
with the knowledge that if I just let go
the dam that holds the river
will dissipate

The Pain of Your Absence

No matter how far I push myself away
It still hurts
Living on this Earth
knowing you're gone...
sometimes becomes too much

Deep Feelings

The memory of you
drips right off my face
I don't understand how an organ can feel
so Damn much

Choices

I chose to hold on after he let go
Finding myself angry with him
that he left so soon
But it wasn't his choice
The choice was selfishly made for him
That is where my anger truly lies

Scribbles 1

There's something about a single tear slowly dripping down one's face that ache's with (a harsh) good-bye

Δ Teαr Filled Hospitαl Room

I stood next to the bed holding your hand
sobbing
I feared you would hear me
but I don't think you could with all those machines
running

Value

People should be valued
more
before they die
Instead
we value them after

Give your flowers
and
share your time
Now
for when they're gone

They're gone forever

Missing You

The pain of the loss
engulfed my whole
Deepening my thoughts
straining my soul
I think of you
your smile
so bright
if I only knew
how soon you'd take flight
To hold your hand
one more time
I would only demand
holding it more
Never wanting to let go
afraid I'll forget
That face that I've come to know
all the time that I've missed
deep inside builds regret

The Doors to Hell

When I walked through those painted double doors
my life was paused
Complete ear ringing silence
For that brief moment
nothing mattered
Nothing

His Eyes

His toddler eyes were always filled with so much wonder and love.

How could anyone want to dim that?

BLU

What were little hands
and little feet
are now replaced with memories
only I can see
My heart
how it aches
My soul
how its turned
This smile
I've learned to fake
I need to amend
everyone's concerns
Such a short life
you were given
I wonder how
I've gone on living
I think of these years
gone by
The things you've missed
 my endless unheard cries
My heart is forever

➜

locked with your pain
Your smile has grown so distant
The world unable to maintain
No matter how hard I wished for it

You are missed more
than words can ever say
Now I come to your grave
I come to where you lay
I loved you then
I love you now
Forever
and always
my beautiful nephew
For I failed to be
your undeniable refuge

Ripped Away

I only held his hand for a short while.
They ripped him from me with such a fierce anger
He never stood a chance.

Loud Silence

The cold steel doors buzz open
stale air fills the space
Frozen in a state of shock I somehow end up
in front of the double doors to hell
Colors and swirls trying to ease the pain
but art can't fix this feeling
My stomach in knots
Static in my head
My heart can't stop fiercely pounding
The cries of loved ones
I'm torn apart
I sit in an overwhelming silence
no words or understanding
I sit there and wait
For something
Anything
Nothing
More silence
Everyone's hugging and crying
but I hear nothing
The doctor comes to explain what's happened   ➥

my hearing still nowhere to be found
When she walked in
with fear in her eyes
suddenly the noise came crashing in
She would not tell me this was all a lie
why wouldn't she wake me up
Instead we head to his room
there my emotions poured to the ground
my heart, too heavy to carry
In that moment I lost a piece of myself
my heart forever damaged

Graveside

I sit at his grave
wind blowing through my hair
It's almost like he's letting me know he's here
Sadness builds as I look upon his marker
Nothing here but a chunk of wood
No final stone to tell me the dates that are already seared
into my brain
Sad pieces of memories lying about the tall grass
A broken bench filled with the weeds of yesterday's

Although he's always with me
coming to this place
I feel him so much more
For this is his final resting place
The amount that I miss this boy
drips from my face
As I lay curled up upon the overgrown grass
allowing for my tears to flow into the Earth
in hopes they may reach him
I'm here
I am always here

Fourteen Year Grief

Digging down deep
to pull out this memory
tears pour from my eyes
I can't seem to bring myself to fully feel it

Sometimes loss lives deep within
in a place you don't know is there
covered in the web of the lies
all saying you're alright
Grief demands to be felt
no matter the lie
or the time
even after fourteen years

Remembering You

The empty day's seem so long
the pain a portion less
Smiling just seems so wrong
death leaves behind a mess

The end can make one feel so alone
Your life now seemed so simple
All the love you've ever shown
surrounds us in this temple

As we say goodbye
we play back our memories
After a good long cry
remembering the good time's
is the best remedy

HER LAST DAYS

She sit's frail and unsteady
her body just isn't her own
For, the end she just isn't ready
to that place before her so many others have flown
Unaccepting of her fate
she fights all the way
To this she wants to be late
She fears she has no say
The confusion takes over like a whirlwind of snow
she tries to take cover but from what she doesn't know
She lays in her bed
holding on tight
Too afraid now
that she might end up seeing the light
The people come and go
as she sits alone
They will never understand
how she yearns to go home
She knows the end is near
but she fights all she can
Shes just not yet ready to go
to the Promised Land

Painful Good-Bye

I held your hand
pushed back your hair
This I cannot stand
This life, so unfair

In the beginning you were so strong
nothing could beat you
When did this all go wrong
if only we really knew

You grew so sick
you grew so sad
This was not the life you picked
I understood why you grew so mad

In the end we all stood by your side
having to let you go
Such a horrible sight
so painful
so slow

Gone

I barely remember
the call I received
or the calls I placed right after
It was the feeling
that placed itself into my memory
The feeling of being worried and scared
Rushing to get there
to be by your side
to hold your hand
through my despair
Arriving in that cold room
seeing you lay there
brought me to my knees
You're the one who had no oxygen
but suddenly I was the one who could not breath
If only I knew in that moment
in less then a week you'd be gone

Dreamland

Lost in a dream so real
lost in another time and place
Is my mind trying to heal
taking me through time and space
I talk to you like you're still here
I can smell all your smells
I feel you so close so near
is this some kind of spell
Waking up to the bitter truth
brings a tear to my eye
I just have to assume
somehow you felt all my cries

Happy Birthday

You werent there for me as a child so our relationship was already cloudy. You hurt me so I stopped talking to you. Then you left. Permanently. Happy Birthday. You're gone and I'm reminiscing about the years we wasted.

CleΔR

The tears build from deep within my soul
pouring from my eyes
This pain in me, I can't control
the fear scarier than I realized

Holding your still hand
my tears continue to fall
None of this I understand
This is not my call

They pull me back
my resistance grows
You've fallen off track
I just froze

As they call out 'CLEAR'
I hold my breath
Just as I feared
Sudden death

ECHO

The roots of dread spread from my lips
overgrowing in the shape of brokenness
The womb no longer lives between my hips
an inner deep loneliness
This emptiness scratches at my webbed soul
despair at every turn
This endless ache takes its toll
understanding patience I must learn
Letting go of this shattered torch
letting emptiness be
The undying truth of all sorts
screams an echoing pain to me

Loss

The loss of the child I never met scratches at my broken
womb
The pain was so hot I yearned for it to be extinguished
With no future of a playroom
he spark was forever diminished

You

I never saw your face
or held your hand
sweet love of mine
The final thoughts
I just cannot stand
The love and loss
combined
Pushing away
the what if's and whys
Pretending everything is ok
I sit alone in my unheard cries
I can't find the right words to say
The life that grew inside of me
may not have been for very long
Now I find myself reminiscing
Wishing for you can't be wrong

To Die For

Death comes to us all
Sometimes even before we die!

CHAPTER 5
SORROW

The disappointment reeks of sorrow

My Eternal Enemy

my
pain
has
been
with
me
longer
than
most
people
have

Melancholy

I'll strip down to my soul
bathing in melancholy
Losing all control
I begin feeling so foggy
These deep pains overcome
fear sets in
Have I become this sadness within?

Death of a Dandelion

The smell of dandelions and dirt dig their way from my
soul
begging to be freed back to the place where they belong
The inner rot feeds on my heart
bringing me to the place I fear the most
As my mind races
the vines of hate spread their dark tangling roots to my
heart
finally devouring my soul
It's too dark for any plant to survive this space
With the holding of tainted breath
small fragile bits of air makes a path
With a gasp, I let it all in
The air
The light
The stench of death
This is the reality
This is where I now live

My Rose

I pluck this dead rose from the ground
thorns digging into my dirt covered chapped hands
We have so much in common
Our petals hunching over from neglect
Our stems crisp from the drought
Our color deep and dark

I hold it there for a moment
grasping my hand closed
I watch what was once beautifully alive
become dust

Taking in the stale air
I blow with a crisp breath
Watching the remnants fly carelessly through the air
brings a calm over my scattered mind
We are as one
As I lay my head down
a swift wind blows
What's left of me
carelessly flies through the air

How

There I was

heart in my hands
tears down my face
silence from my voice
sitting in the filth of denial
regret building up like the climax to a story
shame pouring from my eyes

How?

Heавy

Rigid hands
Cold
Wet
full from the tears they've cupped

Frozen heart
Raw
cracked
Broken from the ice that's concealed
Tormenting thoughts
Stinging yet strong
Throbbing from ideas unreal

This broken feeling grows from an unknown place
demanding to be mended
The heaviness that weighs me down
stay's contended

Hopeless Remembering

The painful past demands to be remembered
My devastation has yet to be severed
So many years just yearning for good
Hopelessness sets in more that it should

FINDING HER OWN INSPIRATION

She sits in her head
sitting in the dark
She's filled with much dread
while searching for a spark

The spark she cant see
it's painfully so distant
She just wants to flee
but she doesn't want to risk it

What is the risk
when she's sitting all alone
She's sitting there so sick
with no place to call home

So sick and so frail
So lonely
So tired
She must start her own trail
she herself can be inspired

Endless Haze

I lay on the floor all broken and bruised
the dirt from my broken soul leaves a dreadful taste
upon my lips
I just stay there on that cold floor letting myself be used
as they take my soul
I allow it to be ripped

Over and over I watch myself disappear
as they enter upon my space
My entire body filled with fear
My hollow heart
finally gone without a trace

Just close my eyes
as they show me their monstrous ways
 Believing all the lies
Living in this endless haze

Finding Me in We

The narcissism runs deep
from the beginning of time
passed down from each generation
They never let my empathy sleep
make my help feel like a crime
leaving me in frustration

Where they start
Do I end?
Where they end
Do I begin?
Pulling away would be smart
getting away from the blend
living this way is a dead end
living this way is a sin

His Drug Of Choice

He spiraled
So much he began to love that neverending winding
chaos
The road to Rock Bottom was his true love
The only home he'll ever know

HeΔLING

They called me a bitch
because I started
to set healthy boundaries

The toxicity dripping from them
clouded them into thinking
I was the problem

Walking away
my problems became light
while their problems remained

I am finally ok
with being the bad guy
My healing is more important
than anything

Drink Your Feelings

You felt insecure so you tipped the bottle back until you forgot why you grabbed it in the first place.

TRUST

There's something in the eyes looking back at me
that I do not trust
Maybe it's all that
pain and sorrow
pretending to be what it is not

MONSTER OF NEGATIVE THOUGHTS

Here comes the confusion again
I'm not sure what's left
what's right
How does this monster get in
always trying to diminish my light

My Funeral

To see unfamiliar faces sitting in still rows
crying over a person they didn't even know
It's confusing and alarming also a bit frustrating
when alive my life was so isolated
No one in sight until my final end
they'll go on with their life after this quick pretend
If I haven't seen you on my breath filled days
please don't show up to watch me decay

Help

Many times I've needed help
but I fear the words can never tell
what I'm feeling when I'm blue
its sad that I can't come and ask you

They say things will get better in time
so then I lie and say I'm fine
Nobody knows just what's the deal
until I break loose and say how I feel

I shouldn't hold in so tight
because it makes me scream with all of my might
So when I lose the ones close to me

My angers to blame
My anger is me

AM I AWAKE?

He calls at 2:30 in the morning
so close to that witching hour that I long for
Reluctantly I answer
No good could come from a call at this time
What is said is only my true nightmare
A man I'm supposed to look up to
A man who would Never treat me like the whores he's
accustomed
But here we are
and just like that
all hope for family is gone
As he talks from a drunken mouth
I let my silence wash over me
consuming the heart he's ripping to shreds
As the poison continues to spill
I simply say good-night
Pinching myself I realize
this
is no dream

The Drowning of My Heart

I kick and throw my hands about
trying to find something to grab onto
My lungs filling up
so I can't even shout
this ending is to soon
Please forgive me for my wrongs
Lightness starts to fill my head
My will no longer strong
I drift away just as the words in my head
I let go of the fight
floating eagerly away
Such a sad sight
Nothing left to say

But Never Settle

I've always wanted more
But sometimes
more is not a good thing

A Seven Years Sadness

Such sad eyes
for a boy so young
He's technical
At times sharp tongued
With the weight of the world
he flashes through life
Sitting in the dark
in all of his strife
If only he could see
all of his greatness
and feel
all of his braveness

When those who are
suppose to protect you
Hurt and leave
no matter what you do
You grow sad eyes
in search of meaning
And spend much of your days
painfully grieving

MY MISTAKE

Their sad eyes
fill me with so much guilt
Their shattered hearts
I try to rebuild
Their suffering
comes from a day I was not there
It isn't right
It's just not fair
My heart pounds
with an ache so fierce
Thinking of that day
fills me with burning tears
Will they ever forgive me
for all of my flaws?
Understand I'm only human
I don't make up the laws
I will continue to
hold on for them
To fill their days with love
to help them find their zen

The Lost Family

Another night filled with hurtful words
full of dismay
The chaos screams loudly in painful hurds
in painful ways
Objects of no use
get thrown through the air
Thrown like our feelings
ricocheting with no care
Fighting for a love
that's right in front of our face
We beg and we plead
We need our own space
Being together
seems impossible
For our feelings
we aren't responsible
Getting away is really what's best
as we've clearly been put through the ultimate test

Sometimes

Sometimes when I sit and cry, I let the tears build up all around me in hopes I'll be carried away on these waves of sadness. Carried away to the place of dreams. Where men aren't forceful and know kindness in their hearts. Where the word Love doesn't leave a bitter taste upon my tongue. A place of beauty that's free of pain and suffering. A place I dream of every night I cry myself to sleep. But the tears drift away quickly, leaving me here in this land of drought. In this place of suffering. All of these tears, yet it's so very dry. I'll forever yearn for this dreamland.

The Catastrophe of my Grief

Maybe the World sets it up so that I never live in my grief. Throwing all these extra obstacles that desire so much of my attention. Knowing that if I let it all out, it will drown cities and rumble mountains. Releasing all this sadness at once could be catastrophic.

WOUNDS UNSEEN

Sitting with such wonder in my head
the times ticking away
I want to escape all of my regrets
I fear I have nothing left to say
The wounds show from under my skin
My reflection has abruptly changed
This race against life no one can win
This race leaves us with nothing to gain
With all my sorrows answered
I'm less likely to see the light
I give in to this cancer
I have nothing for which to fight

To the unforeseen circumstances

To the ugliness and rotten glances

To the hatred hidden behind untrue words

To the safeness found in the sound of records

To the heart that feels shattered and sore

To those who just can't take anymore

- YOU ARE FINE

Vulnerable Soul

And there I go again
Pouring out my soul
being left
open and vulnerable

THE BALANCE IN HER SOUL

The pain takes over
Black lines running down her face
finding themselves pooling at her chin
searching for what drove her to this
Those dark tears came from a darker place inside of her
A sweet smell of brokenness pours from her composure
as she searches the room in her soul for anything that
doesn't take over
Her spirit a mess she acts as if she's not a pushover
just looking for what will get her closer
to a life that doesn't throw her
to a life that knows her
to one that wont expose her
These painful days are for no amateur
One day she'll find her balancer
in a wonderful atmosphere
She wont let herself disappear
into that dark stale air
made of nightmares

THE WILL OF MY WORDS

The pain behind my words will remain
my pain that's so very deep
I'll write out all of my shame
for these words are my place to weap

In this moment my World stands still
the hurt drools onto the paper
My secret now forever spilled
from this I try not to waver

Let out all my secrets
my demons
my darkness
No more space for
chaos and weakness
Making room for
a hopeful calmness

Painful Memory

The stale air clutched at my throat, a stabbing in my chest. I fell to the floor cupping my hand over my heart as if I could hold onto all of the pain I was feeling. I didn't want it spilling over and engulfing me entirely. As I struggle to catch my breath, a deep gasp overcomes. The reality of the situation hit me like a ton of bricks. So heavy. So hard. There was nothing in the air. No hand around my throat. I'm the one in control. As the air fills my lungs, a smile creates. How close I was to letting a simple memory take my life.

LUNCHTIME SADNESS

A deep sadness fills my already busy mind
the clock sounds of noon
I grab my glass and fill it full with this bitter wine
I always pair it with my mood

The thoughts flood in as I try to forget
I just cant allow myself
I wash them away with each little sip
all while I sit judging myself

The more and more that I consume
helps me to hide the guilt
One can only assume
that I truly love the life that I've built

Sadness followed by regret
Emptiness and sorrow
Living life feeling upset
only takes away the hope of tomorrow

LEFT WITH MY LONELY SELF

What happens continuously shapes me to who I am
All the lies I've been told
All the heartache that unfolds
All of this life so cold
Left with nothing to hold

Scribbles 2

You cannot talk sense to a senseless person. Sometimes walking away is the best option. Something I've become great at! I know I'm not perfect. I know my flaws and faults but I also know my worth.

LOSING MY TRUST

It's not easy
Trusting people

I opened up to them and they exploited me
thinking my emotions were theirs to play
If only they could see
Once my trust is gone
they'll never see it again

JUST LIKE A TEAPOT

I was blocked from feeling
After a rainfall of emotions I'm now in a drought
When the teapot screams for so long
even her water dries up

Another Tragic Poem

another painful day
painful in so many ways
ways so hard to express
the expression turns to a depression

another tragedy to go at alone
all alone even with a full home
a home that feels so broken
the brokeness has turned to loneliness

another poem to write
write about all the pain in sight
this sight is growing so dim
with the dimness that remains within

Sadness Within

I've become the sadness within the sadness

That of which began as a little girl

Trying so hard to not become this

But here I am

feeling it

everyday

every minute

I don't know how to get through

for I just want to give up

This roaring strength in me says I can't

A grief like I've never known

A pain I can't shake

It's way too much for any human to hold

Before it explodes

Before I explode

Taking a deep breath

letting out all of the pain

the fury

the hatred

I now bury them

with the strength that was hidden within

Finally I can breathe

Δ Meaning Fulfilled

Staring down at this blank paper

I'm tired

How do I describe a feeling so indescribable

a pain that's so deep

How do I put into words

how I let myself be treated so poorly by the men that

say they love me

while showing the opposite

How do I explain to my daughter

that not all men are this way

even though this is all we've ever known

How do I put it all out there for the judges to judge

For the weapers to weap

For the lonely heartbroken to see they are not alone

Suddenly the blank paper is filled

I've described the indescribable

I've brought meaning to the meaningless

I've given fire for the judges

paper to wipe away tears of heartbreak

and a place for comfort

All nestled deep within the words

scribbled atop invisible lines

Highway Emotions

Emotions
Rushing through like a speeding car with no destination
Once they hit 100
they start feeling unstable
150
They're losing it
200
They spin out
Emotions
Funny little things
If not driven correctly
crash

THE MIX OF WATER AND TEARS

Tears drip like a heavy rainstorm
while I feel my worth
Standing in this shower
to quiet the pain
the heaviness of my chest
starts to get the best of me
I try to wash it all away
Something about the water washing over me
gives such a comfort
More than I've received
from myself
or any other
As I watch the tears
and water mix together
I say goodbye
as they swirl down the drain
in perfect harmony
one in the same

The Rupture From Within

It's been quiet for so long
The pressure building up
so intense
so strong
Get ready for the wind-up
This sudden deep release
comes from deep within
The momentum will only increase
if she pushes it back in
The inner rupture of her earthquake
has her shaking to her core
Keeping her afraid
she just couldn't take anymore
So with an open mouth
she releases all the pain
With screams so loud
she saves herself from the insane

The Wrong Always Fall

Oh how the tides have turned
your getting what you deserve
To many people you have burned
my whole heart included
Say whatever you want to say
it never mattered anyway
Stop and see what you have been doing
only a few you have been fooling

SCRIBBLES 3

Things change in a heartbeat
Decisions you make
Hearts you break
Time you take

Are You Projecting

I hurt your feelings by speaking My truth?
Why don't you ask yourself why my authenticity hurt's
you so damn much!
My opinions are just that
Mine
I will never apologize for living my truth

Scribbles 4

It was in my death
that I finally opened my eyes to living

The Girl with the Heart of Loss

She walks with her head weighed down
She talks in a quiet tone
She holds onto that tired frown
Love is something she's never been shown

The pain
she wears on her face
The loss
she carries everywhere
Her family gone without a trace
She feels that life is so unfair

Left behind with only the bag on her back
She's been left alone to fend
Finding difficulty staying on track
 Being ok is so hard to pretend

➜

This secret pain she carries within
sometimes lashes out on those near
New relationships are so hard to begin
when she's living everyday in fear

of losing the ones she loves so deep
as she's lost so many before
Alone she sits to weap
Love feels like a war

Scribbles 5

Have I brought on all this chaos
making sure my inner peace never sparks
Have I torn these painful memories
from a place that's so very dark
To live here in this moment
feeling overwhelmed
insecure...
Why I live this way
sits in my mind
I'm just so deeply unsure

STRIFE

The truth lays across my darkened soul
The pain that lies beyond the unknown
I drift away to a place so still
But instantly brought back against my will
When will the choice ever be mine
To leave this loud chaos behind
To be still and open to a fulfilling life
Not to be held back
and full of strife

Not as it Seems

This dark painful day never seems to end
I search for my escape
Looking around at these soulless friends
nothing left besides hate

To have such hate there must be more
more feelings then just dark
For this I'll have to really explore
what came before this mark

How do I find something besides this pain
a love that is so strong
Maybe it washes away just like the rain
perhaps I got it all wrong

The Telling of Secrets

My head
cluttered
filled to the brim
if I pack in so much
I won't have to worry about feeling
Boy, am I ever wrong
but I'll continue to take it all in
that's what I'm good at
overthinking and underdoing
Alone with only my thoughts

Thoughts, so congested
it's hard having just one
Exhaustion overcomes
and I give in
I disclose
Letting my thoughts drip from my tongue
With each drip
translucence
Finally
a silence →

It Silences the thoughts I once believed
I was so comfortable with
It Silences the fears of having
one thought at a time
Silence will become my best friend
But sometimes
friends are not as they appear
Always finding out too late
that they were never my friends
but covered in disguise
My enemies
Enemies that now hold
all of my secrets

CHAPTER 6
BETRAYAL

It starts with trust
Then ends in betrayal

Breaking Ties

Everyone I spoke to
took advantage of my pain
I had nowhere to run to
this pain would always remain

To the family to who I cried
who laughed at my demise
while I was being denied
your truth came alive

To the highschool guidance that broke down my walls
then told everyone my story
making me feel so fucking small
began my path of fury

Trust after trust I gave
only to be knocked on my ass
making me fear's slave
so long that would last

➜

One day I would be used
but this time I'll realize
No longer am I willing to be abused
I'll break these unhealthy ties

Keeping my truths to myself
until the time was right
began my journey of healing oneself
it built my will to fight

Sharing Secrets

I share my secret stories
out of order of course
one can only imagine
how many nights were spent crying on the floor

digging up the past
the moments that wish to stay deep down
fills my head with pain
tears falling to the ground

my stomach left in knots
as I begin to share
wishing I could write
about more than just despair

I can only write what I know
as sad as it is
from my mouth drips the truth
the truth of unheard sins

Pushing Through

So many memories
fill my busy brain
From friends to enemies
sane to insane

Moments so true
then fake as can be
Sometimes so blue
the light unable to be seen

I continue to try
no matter the cost
With a little sigh
I push through all that I've lost

No, Taken Lightly

He called me a tease
and continued with his curious hands
Hungry for pleasure
calling out demands
My tears puddled behind my head
as I wished for it to end
He finished with me
no sign of amends
"What's the matter with you?"
"Really, it's not like you didn't want it."
"Quit throwing a fit."
I broke my voice repeating No
as he was breaking my soul
He walked away without a care
leaving me
Never able to replace what he stole

The Pathological Family

The lies
unnecessary
but they tell them anyway
Putting themselves
high on a pedestal
Making others cry
was their forte
Their cruelness
unforgettable
Even as time moves on
this behavior
so unacceptable
How do they care not
for their wrongs
Their cruelness ricochets
right back to where it belongs

The Conceited 'Friend'

I was struggling with life
so I opened up to her
The 'friend' that always counted on me
I needed for a moment to refer

Her ugliness shown
Her hateful words stabbed
The resentment so strong
this didn't go as planned

Her pretending to care now gone
For I was no longer needed
How blind I had been
For she was secretly conceited

CHAOS CHASERS

It's strange how many curious souls show up in the
middle of your chaos..
Count the ones who stay when the chaos ends.

Take No Shit

I have so many layers
and
Every single one of them
does **Not** want to put up with your shit

R B F

Call me a fucking Bitch
like it'll ruin my day!
I'll give the best resting bitch face
you'll ever see!

Chapter 7
MOVING FORWARD

Sometimes the only choice that is left after going

through so much pain and loss, is moving forward.

The Rain

I sit and listen to the rain hit the ground
it's washing away the day
In this moment I dive into the sound
this rain
it has so much to say

With each drop I feel the weight lifting off
the invisible weight that I carry
It feels like the rain is just enough
it's deep thunder unearths all that I've buried

I walk out under those non judgemental drops
just letting it all wash away
I stand there until my unhealthy thoughts stop
these thoughts always have so much to say

Harder and harder it streams down my face
the bitter cold reminds me I'm alive
It washes away and then leaves without a trace
taking my brain into an utter dive

→

I dive into my purpose
my meaning to it all
Washing away the surface
help's realize I can get up after I fall

Breaking Down my Walls

I spent so long building my walls that I never understood why it was so dark and nothing would grow. After I began knocking them down, letting light and warmth in, everything started to grow and I quickly was surrounded by life.

I Hope

I hope there is meaning to how much
my heart is aching right now

Hurting Out Loud

I never understood this anger I have
until now
It's the reflection of
just how hurt I am
screaming out loud
demanding attention
Finally understanding
I stop starving it
Allowing the anger to express itself
has brought me an unguilty peace
Hurting out loud
has silenced the inner pain

Open-Close

When this house fills with the smoke of hate, I can sit here with it allowing it to suffocate my very being or I can open the door and release that negative shit out into the atmosphere to where it belongs. Either way, the choice is mine!

Scribbles 6

Looking back brings pain

                    Living in the past makes the day small

Looking forward brings joy

              Living in the now makes the day feel endless

SCRIBBLES 7

Another positive quote
diving deep into what I wrote
to try to ease these deep pains
These are my attempts to try to stay sane

Scribbles 8

Looking for my light
I must enter the dark
With the foresight
I ignite the spark

REALIZATION

With both hands clenched into fists, I beat the ground, as if it was mother nature's fault for all of this pain I've been dealt. I learned quickly, when you throw blame around and don't take responsibility for yourself, mother nature has a tendency to bite back! So I sat and sobbed with two extremely pain-filled and slowly bruising hands. With all of this trouble still sitting with me. I don't know what I thought. Maybe pounding the ground was going to all of a sudden make everything better. Maybe sobbing about it was going to make it all just disappear. Then, I let it go. I started to feel better. I allowed Mother Earth's bite to awaken me. I let her in. There's a lesson in the pain. There's a lesson in throwing blame. Learning those lessons leads you to the beauty of LIfe. In taking responsibility, in being open, in being honest. True Beauty.

WALK THROUGH THE DOOR

The day I stopped blaming others and took responsibility
was the day I realized the prison I was in
had an open door
this whole time

Overcome with Numbing Thoughts

Looking for my light
I must enter the dark
With the foresight
I ignite the spark

Something just isn't right
I'm feeling so broken
so numb
In search of some kind of light
looking for my meaning to come

Sitting here deep in my thoughts
the pain just can't escape
Beautiful is something it's not
It has taken most all of my shape

Igniting the spark so bright
I now see what's to be seen
Engulfing in light
Now comfortable with the in between

My Helping Heart

Please take my hand
as we walk this path together
I may never have a plan
but can withstand any weather
My passion runs so deep
that I feel it in my soul
High emotions I can't keep
I find my way through loopholes
The intensity may sting
but I promise it will be worth it
To the table I have so much to bring
just be ready for the conversion

Move Forward

As the water hits my skin
the emotions hit the floor
Wash away these sins
I don't want them anymore
If to get through my days
leaving the past behind
I must awaken from this haze
stop pressing rewind
So I'll let it wash over me
I let it soak in
I'll finally be able to see
high emotions don't always win

LONELY RAIN

In the rain I find comfort in my loneliness
the simplicity of the staggering drops brings familiarity
My soul has been stuck inharmonious
this rain creates my clarity

It May Never Come

There's never enough time when you wait until tomorrow

Finding Peace in a Stranger

I never planned to tell you
the secrets of my past
You brought them out of me
easier then I could have guessed
How easy to trust a stranger
who I'll never meet again
I poured it all out as you poured the wine
letting you fully in
That night cherished forever
how judgemental you were not
Never have I missed a stranger
Peace for me was what you brought

Repeat

Sometimes
when I don't listen
My lessons live on repeat
until I do

BORN FOR THIS

As the sun pierces my skin
I begin to see
the life that I'm living
the peace in front of me
The beauty of today
is right within reach
If I only follow it
not allowing it to be breached
Most times
I allow the chaos to flood in
I just don't see
how I allow the chaos to win
I have to move forward
push through all the hurts
This sitting in silence
only makes matters worse
I have the strength
the power
the will
I can do anything
I was born to fulfill

Darkness

The waves crash down
like the pain inside of my heart
With my eyes open wide
I can't see without the dark
The darkness has always
been there for me
It's the only thing
that never leaves
So when you think
you can't go on without the shining bit of light
Look at this darkness
as your undoubtable will to fight

Taking Fate into her Hands

"I won't wait for things to stop being hard, to live a life I Love!"
She says with a matchbox in one hand and sunglasses on, watching the bridges go up in flames!

Δ Fresh Coat of Paint

Yesterday
I rebuilt my walls
and held back my tears

Today
I'm busting those useless things down
and letting those tears flow

Δ Soul that is Whole

You reminded me that I am more
More than the pain and sadness within
You helped me reach down to my inner core
knowing that I am not just an empty sin

I wanted the other half of my soul
The love that I thought existed
But you showed me that I am a whole
Together we don't have to risk it

I have my strength and my will
You stand right beside me
I just can't wait until
I can show you how much you have helped me

Scribbles 9

There's a beautiful stillness in the rushing of waves that cover's my heart in hope

From Lioness to her inner Cub

Your mourning
will not last forever
Your tainted cries
will evaporate like a waterless river

This discomfort you feel every single day
you will turn it around
to strengthen you in your own incredible ways

Right now you wonder
Why is this happening?
You feel so lost
it's all very maddening

But I can tell you it's all going to be ok!
You will stand tall!
Your voice
such a wonderful discovery

→

Your story may now
be painful and sad
But the future holds promise
Those feelings leave a lot to be said

So today may be tough
with many crosses to bare
Just remember this little cub
Your strength has been
and always will be
there!

Scribbles 10

And then I realized I would never fully heal while holding
onto all of my hurts.
So I let them all go...

Letting Go and Moving Forward

these words I have wrote
I let them go
they hold no power over me anymore

I finish this book
on a strong note
like a bird I soar

I open space
for healing
open my mind
and heart
to continue feeling

everything lay in front of me
I embrace
I am ready

To all those I have loved so fierce

To all those who have hurt me

Thank you for all you have shown me

Also by me

The Scribbles of a Broken Heart

Regina Ducey

Being born under a First Quarter moon with a sun sign of Aquarius and a moon sign of Taurus, makes for quite the contradictory personality. I live in a small village in Upstate NY, raising my two amazing children. You can find me sipping tea through the chaos of life while trying to make every moment count.